Beginn(
Crystal Reports 2016
A Quick Start Guide

Use for Versions XI, 2008, 2011, 2013 and 2016

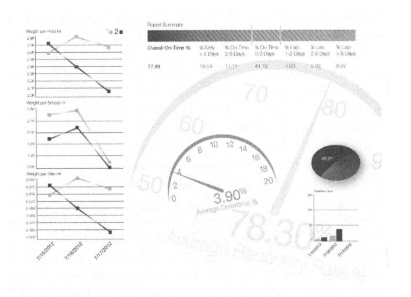

Fourth Edition

Eric M. Gatmaitan

About the Author

Eric M. Gatmaitan earned a master in business administration degree with an emphasis on business information systems from Western Michigan University and a bachelor of science degree in industrial management engineering with a minor in mechanical engineering from De La Salle University.

Mr. Gatmaitan was a faculty member instructing classes in computer technology application, systems analysis & design and programming for the Business Information Systems department in the College of Business at Western Michigan University. In the healthcare manufacturing industry, he served as an Industrial Engineer, Production Supervisor, Plant Manager, and Chief Operating Officer.

As a management consultant, Mr. Gatmaitan leads projects and conducts training in the areas of strategic planning, business-process optimization, quality systems, and performance management systems.

ISBN-10:154697296X
ISBN-13: 978-1546972969

Table of Contents

Table of Contents

Introduction

The contents of this book are useful for learning Crystal Reports versions XI, 2008, 201, 2013, and 2016. This book was written as a quick start guide for beginners, and not intended as a reference manual. The beginner-level skills of Crystal Reports is easy to learn and can be achieved within a few hours of hands-on learning. Crystal Reports also contains advanced features that will challenge programmers and technical users.

This book is formatted as a work instruction for readers to follow and learn-by-doing. It is highly recommended that Crystal Reports be installed and the example Microsoft® Access database Xtreme.mdb downloaded for the reader to follow the step-by-step guide. Use a web browser and type "*Microsoft® Access EXTREME.MDB*" to locate and download the filename Xtreme.mdb. A trial version of Crystal Reports is also available from SAP Data Objects.

There are two sets of users for Crystal Reports, they are Report Viewers and Report Developers. Report Viewers are those who access existing Crystal Report files (*.rpt) and execute the file to produce the report. Report Developers, on the other hand, create report templates that define the data connection, columns of data, calculations, summary data and report parameters. Reports with advanced features will require Report Developers to have some knowledge of programming fundamentals.

Crystal Reports is intended for Report Developers only. Report users will only need a "Crystal Viewer", a free software available at the web for download. Crystal Viewers are software utilities designed to run report with parameter options. Crystal Viewers doesn't have the capabilities to alter the design details of the report such as format or formulas.

User proficiency increases each time a new report is developed. It is best to approach the learning process incrementally and explore one feature at a time. There are so many features to learn in Crystal Reports, take time to document each new feature learned using a note taking software such as Microsoft® One Note. Aside from the Help feature built within Crystal Reports, an abundant number of tips and tricks are also available at the web. An extensive user guide is available from SAP, web search "SAP Crystal Reports 2016 User Guide" to download the user guide.

This book is intended to provide the reader with the basic skills in creating simple reports and the confidence to continue learning advanced skills independently.

Chapter 1: Accessing a New Data Source

Setting up a data connection is the only hurdle at learning and using Crystal Reports. This chapter is intended for Accounting, ERP, or MRP systems using a back-end data source such as SQL. Connecting to Microsoft® Excel and Microsoft® Access data files is much simpler as outlined in Chapter 3.

IT support may be required to perform the one-time initial setup of the data connection such as the ODBC data connection to a secure server location. For PC's to access SQL data sources, download and install the latest free version of Microsoft® SQL Server® Express with Tools. The download and installation file will include SQL Management Studio, a utility for intermediate users to create custom view tables.

Once a PC or user terminal is setup with the data connection, the report developer can freely create reports without fear of compromising system data.

Preparing a Server or PC

1. Select **My Computer.**

2. Select **C:** drive.

3. Select **Windows.**

4. Select **System32** for 32-bit PC's or **SysWOW64** for 64-bit PC's.

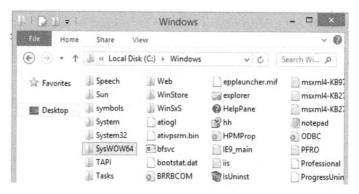

5. Launch **obdcad32** application.

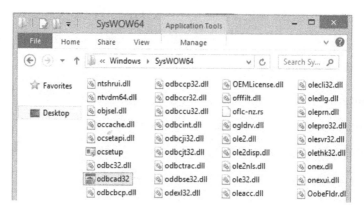

6. Select **User DSN** or **System DSN** tab. Consult with your IT service provider for guidance.

7. Select **Add** to launch the Create New Data Source window.

8. Select **Data Source type.**

9. Select **Finish.**

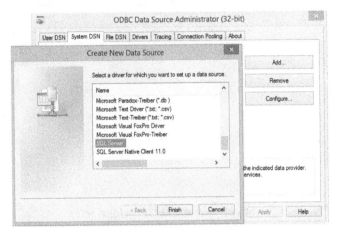

10. Enter **Name** to reference the data connection setup.

11. Enter **Description** of database.

12. Select or type the **Server Name**. See System Administrator for Server Name.

13. Select **Next.**

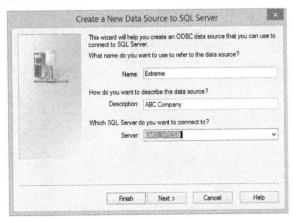

14. Contact your IT Service provider for network permissions.

15. Select **Next** to verify data connection setup.

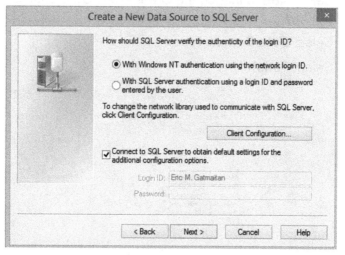

16. Check "Change the default database to".

17. Select **data source** from pull-down menu.

18. Select **Next.**

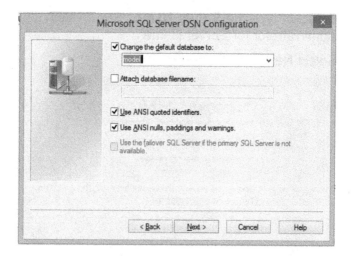

19. Select **Finish.**

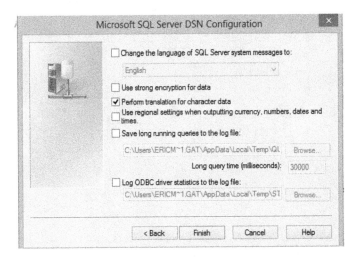

20. Select **Test Data Source** to test the connection.

21. Select **OK** to exit SQL Server ODBC Data Source Test. Consult with an IT service provider if test connection fails.

22. Select **OK** to exit data connection setup window.

23. Select **OK** to exit.

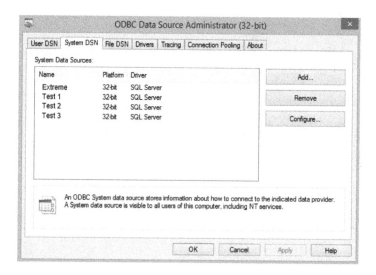

Tip: View System Type in Windows® 8

1. **Point to lower left-hand corner** of the Start or Desktop screen.

2. **Right-mouse click.**

3. Select **System.**

4. Locate **System Type.**

Tip: View System Type in Windows® 10

1. Go to the Windows 10 start menu.

2. Type **System Information.**

3. Select **System Information.**

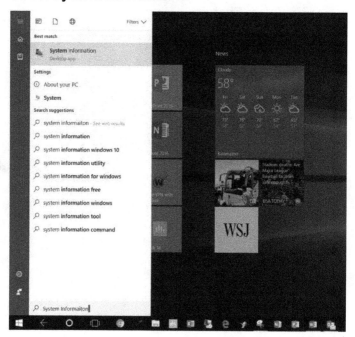

4. Locate **System Type.**

Chapter 2: Understanding the Data Structure

Front-end Application and Back-end Database

Computer applications, such as ERP, MRP and accounting systems, are developed in two segments. The front-end application contains the programming codes, and the back-end contains the data tables and view tables. A view table, also known as a query table, is a combination of data fields from multiple data tables.

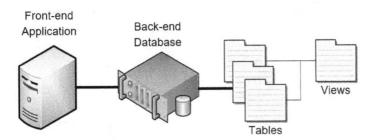

Data Access

Developers of ERP systems and accounting systems embed Crystal Reports© as part of the software. Most often, system software will have a utility to add custom reports to be launched from within the application.

Having the option to access multiple data sources enables a report developer to merge data from an ERP system, production system, accounting system and even a spreadsheet. This feature opens up a lot of options for data collection, reporting, and analysis.

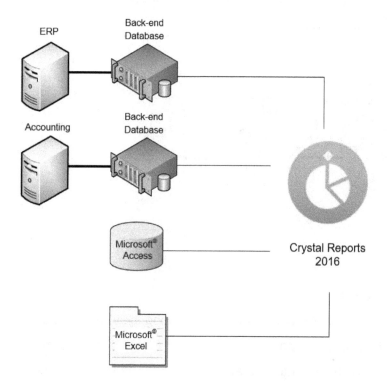

Definition of Terms

Field: Single data element.

Record: Collection of data fields.

Table: A collection of records.

View: A compilation of multiple data tables.

Database: A collection of data tables and views.

Key field: Select field(s) that bind data tables in a database and is used to index a database for fast data retrieval.

Database Index: A data structure that improves the search and access of records.

Direct Access: The process of obtaining data directly with the aid of indexed fields. This data collection process is quicker than sequential access where it evaluates each data record and determines if the data is required.

Note: A Microsoft® Access database file named Xtreme.mdb is used as a data source in this book. The sample database file is available via the web by typing "*Xtreme.mdb sample database*" on a search browser.

Learning and Understanding the Database Structure

1. Get a list of data tables and views. If not available, contact the software developer or request the IT Service Provider to extract the database structure. Shown below is a portion of the Table Structure of Xtreme.mdb listing the table (i.e. Accounts) and the data fields (i.e. Account Number).

Applied IE Table Structure for Xtreme.mdb — Page 1 of 10

Account

Name	Type	Size
Account Number	Short Text	8
Account Heading Number	Short Text	8
Account Type ID	Integer	2
Account Class ID	Integer	2
Account Name	Short Text	50
Description	Short Text	100
Account Balance	Currency	8

Account Class

Name	Type	Size
Account Class ID	Integer	2
Account Class	Short Text	50

Account Heading

Name	Type	Size
Account Heading Number	Short Text	8
Account Heading Name	Short Text	50

Account Type

Name	Type	Size
Account Type ID	Integer	2
Account Type	Short Text	20

Bill

Name	Type	Size
Bill #	Long Integer	4
Vendor Name	Short Text	50
Statement Date	Date With Time	8
Paid Date	Date With Time	8
Gross Amount	Currency	8
Paid	Yes/No	1
Tax	Currency	8

2. Review the data table and view names.

    a. Examine the data fields on each table and view.

    b. Examine the data type and comments.

    c. Note the key fields on each data table. Key fields on each table are important when creating reports using multiple tables. The key fields bind multiple data tables to quickly generate the report. Non-key fields can also be used to bind tables and will result in slower report generation.

3. Identify data table(s) needed for a report.

    a. Identify the least number of data tables and/or views.

    b. View tables, being processed query files, may contain the data you need in a single file.

Chapter 3: Starter Level Skills

Creating a New Report with a New Data Connection

1. **Launch** SAP Crystal Reports.

2. Select **File.**

3. Select **New.**

4. Select **Standard Report.**

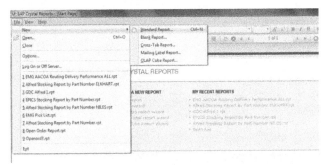

5. Select "**+**" next to **Create New Connection** to view options.

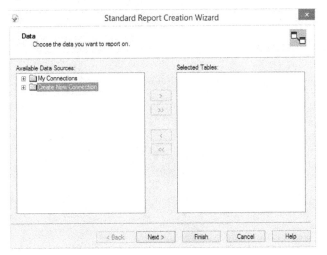

6. Select "**+**" next to **Access/Excel (DAO)** to expand options.

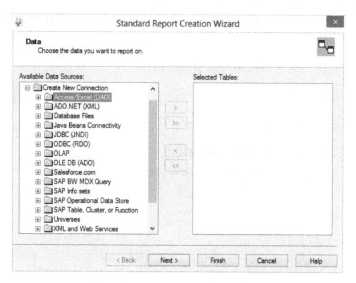

7. Select **Database Name** by clicking on the icon.

8. **Navigate** to the target folder.

9. Select the filename "**Xtreme**" or the target database name to access.

10. Select **Open.**

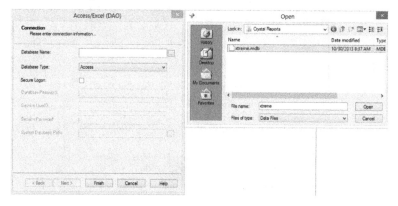

11. Make sure the Database type is **Access.**

12. Select **Finish.**

Selecting Tables for a Report

1. Expand the Data Source **Xtreme.mdb** by selecting the "+" sign next to the file path location.

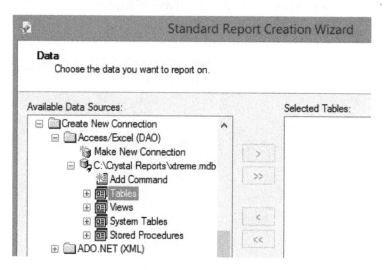

2. **Expand** the table folder by selecting the "+" sign next to Tables.

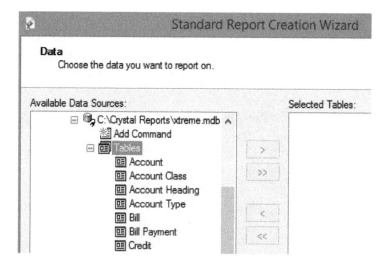

3. Select the table **Orders.**

4. Click on the ">" to copy the selected table name.

5. Select **Finish** when done.

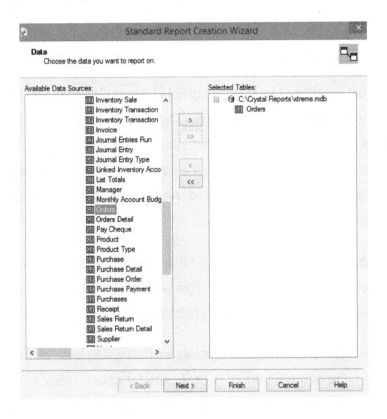

Introduction to Report Sections

In this chapter, the reader will start creating simple reports listing data records in a column and progress at creating summary reports as described in Chapter 7.

Definition of Terms

Report Header : Data, text or graphic items placed in this section will only appear once at Page 1. This section is best used for large reports where basic report information is located, such as the company logo, report title or date range. The succeeding pages of the report are allocated mostly for column data and charts.

Report Footer: Items placed in this section will appear only once at the last page of the report. This section is best used for a report summary, such as report totals or charts.

Page Header: Items placed in this section will appear at the top of each page of the report. It is best used for column headers or field titles. When creating a summary report, the report headers are placed in this section. Items in this section will not show on "drill-down" data sections.

Page Footer: Items placed in this section appear at the bottom of each page. It can contain items such as page number, filename, print date or print time.

Details: This section displays the data records and formulas. Format of each field can customized, and data fields for a single record can be positioned in multiple rows. For summary reports, this section can be set to "Hide (Drill-Down OK)" as an option for a user to expand a summary row to reveal the detailed data.

Group Header: This section by default contains the group name field. It is displayed on top of each set of data. For summary reports, this section is best used to contain the "drill-down" data headers or field titles. When this section is properly set to "Hide (Drill-Down OK)", this section will expand when a user drills down on a summary line item to view the Details section.

Group Footer: This section usually contains group summary items such as totals or averages. It is located below the Details section. For summary reports, the Group Name field is moved to this section.

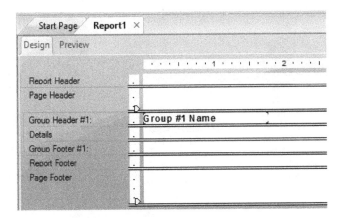

Adding Fields to a Report Detail

1. Open Field Explorer.
   a. Select **View.**
   b. Select **Field Explorer or** Click on **Field Explorer icon.**

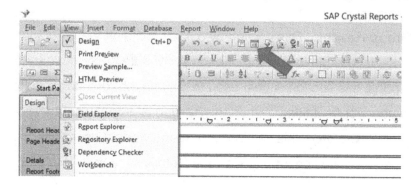

2. Click on the "**+**" to expand the **Database Field** and view the available tables.

3. Click on the "**+**" next to the *Orders* table and view the available fields .

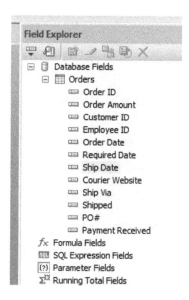

4. Drag the fields *Order ID, Order Amount, Customer ID, Order Date* and *Ship Date* to the Details section.

   Note: Text field names will automatically be placed on the Page Header section.

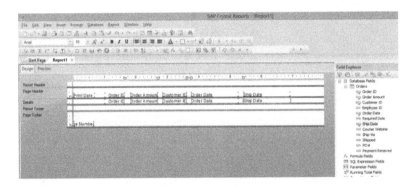

5. Click on **Preview** to view live data.

   Note: Crystal Reports© is a report utility with READ-ONLY authority .

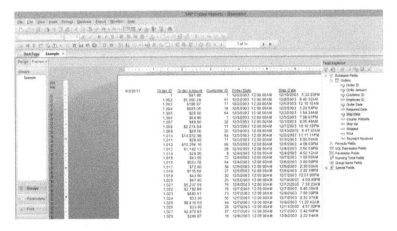

Chapter 4: Basic Formatting of Report

Formatting Data Fields

1. Right-mouse click on the data field to format.

2. Select **Format Field.**

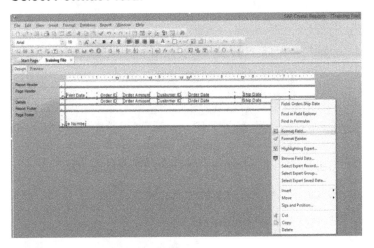

3. Select the format **Style.**

4. Select **OK** when done.

Adding a Group to a Report

1. Click on **Report.**

2. Select **Group Expert.**

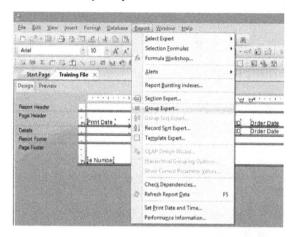

3. Select the field name ***Orders.Cutomer ID*** to Group.

4. Click on "**>**" to copy field name.

5. Select **OK** when done.

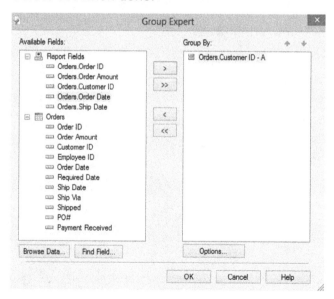

6. Notice *Group #1 Name* label in the Design view.

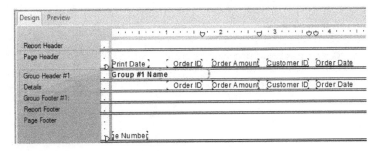

7. Select **Preview** to view report.

8. Notice the new report format with Group.

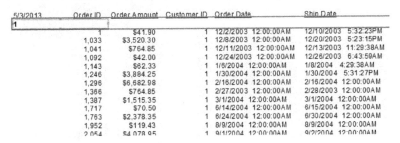

9. Clean-up Details section, if necessary.

10. Select **Design.**

11. Clean-up Details section, if necessary. To remove a field, select the field and press the **Delete** key.

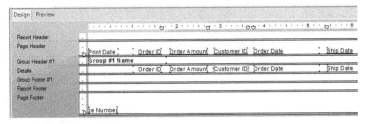

12. Select **Preview** to view report.

5/3/2013	Order ID	Order Amount	Order Date	Ship Date
1				
	1	$41.90	12/2/2003 12:00:00AM	12/10/2003 5:32:23PM
	1,033	$3,520.30	12/8/2003 12:00:00AM	12/20/2003 5:23:15PM
	1,041	$764.85	12/11/2003 12:00:00AM	12/13/2003 11:29:38AM
	1,092	$42.00	12/24/2003 12:00:00AM	12/26/2003 6:43:59AM
	1,143	$62.33	1/6/2004 12:00:00AM	1/8/2004 4:29:38AM
	1,246	$3,884.25	1/30/2004 12:00:00AM	1/30/2004 5:31:27PM
	1,296	$6,682.98	2/16/2004 12:00:00AM	2/16/2004 12:00:00AM
	1,366	$764.85	2/27/2003 12:00:00AM	2/28/2003 12:00:00AM
	1,387	$1,515.35	3/1/2004 12:00:00AM	3/1/2004 12:00:00AM
	1,717	$70.50	6/14/2004 12:00:00AM	6/15/2004 12:00:00AM
	1,763	$2,378.35	6/24/2004 12:00:00AM	6/30/2004 12:00:00AM
	1,952	$119.43	8/9/2004 12:00:00AM	8/9/2004 12:00:00AM
	2,054	$4,078.95	9/1/2004 12:00:00AM	9/2/2004 12:00:00AM
	2,142	$46.50	9/25/2004 12:00:00AM	10/6/2004 12:00:00AM
	2,167	$75.80	9/30/2004 12:00:00AM	9/30/2004 12:00:00AM
	2,277	$122.65	10/27/2004 12:00:00AM	10/31/2004 12:00:00AM
	2,337	$68.00	11/7/2004 12:00:00AM	11/13/2004 12:00:00AM
	2,402	$185.20	11/22/2004 12:00:00AM	11/23/2004 12:00:00AM
	2,528	$136.47	12/24/2004 12:00:00AM	12/24/2004 12:00:00AM
	2,640	$2,939.85	1/26/2005 12:00:00AM	1/26/2005 12:00:00AM
	2,659	$659.70	1/30/2005 12:00:00AM	2/1/2005 12:00:00AM
	2,682	$931.05	2/2/2005 12:00:00AM	2/4/2005 12:00:00AM
	2,687	$27.00	2/4/2005 12:00:00AM	2/10/2005 12:00:00AM
	2,772	$2,294.55	2/28/2005 12:00:00AM	3/5/2005 12:00:00AM
	2,900	$5,549.40	4/9/2005 12:00:00AM	4/16/2005 12:00:00AM
	2,982	$63.90	4/29/2005 12:00:00AM	5/2/2005 12:00:00AM
2				
	1,145	$27.00	1/6/2004 12:00:00AM	1/17/2004 6:33:11PM
	1,171	$479.85	1/14/2004 12:00:00AM	1/14/2004 2:39:50AM
	1,233	$139.48	1/27/2004 12:00:00AM	1/29/2004 1:12:05PM
	1,254	$2,497.05	2/3/2004 12:00:00AM	2/4/2004 3:51:39PM
	1,256	$70.50	2/4/2004 12:00:00AM	2/4/2004 9:27:33AM
	1,288	$8,819.55	2/12/2004 12:00:00AM	2/12/2004 12:00:00AM

Sorting Data Records in the Details Section

1. Select **Report.**

2. Select **Record Sort Expert.**

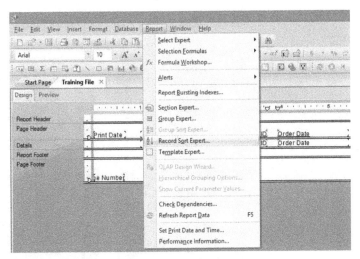

3. Select the field *Orders.Order Date* to sort.

4. Select ">" to copy the field name to the Sort Fields.

5. Select **Ascending** or **Descending.**

6. Select **OK** when done.

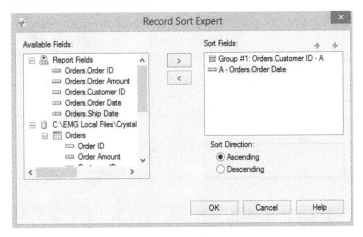

7. Select **Preview** to view the report.

	Order ID	Order Amount	Order Date	Ship Date
5/3/2013				
1				
	1,366	$764.85	2/27/2003 12:00:00AM	2/28/2003 12:00:00AM
	1	$41.90	12/2/2003 12:00:00AM	12/10/2003 5:32:23PM
	1,033	$3,520.30	12/8/2003 12:00:00AM	12/20/2003 5:23:15PM
	1,041	$764.85	12/11/2003 12:00:00AM	12/13/2003 11:29:38AM
	1,092	$42.00	12/24/2003 12:00:00AM	12/26/2003 6:43:59AM
	1,143	$62.33	1/6/2004 12:00:00AM	1/8/2004 4:29:38AM
	1,246	$3,884.25	1/30/2004 12:00:00AM	1/30/2004 5:31:27PM
	1,296	$6,682.98	2/16/2004 12:00:00AM	2/16/2004 12:00:00AM
	1,387	$1,515.35	3/1/2004 12:00:00AM	3/1/2004 12:00:00AM
	1,717	$70.50	6/14/2004 12:00:00AM	6/15/2004 12:00:00AM
	1,763	$2,378.35	6/24/2004 12:00:00AM	6/30/2004 12:00:00AM
	1,952	$119.43	8/9/2004 12:00:00AM	8/9/2004 12:00:00AM
	2,054	$4,078.95	9/1/2004 12:00:00AM	9/2/2004 12:00:00AM
	2,142	$46.50	9/25/2004 12:00:00AM	10/6/2004 12:00:00AM
	2,167	$75.80	9/30/2004 12:00:00AM	9/30/2004 12:00:00AM
	2,277	$122.65	10/27/2004 12:00:00AM	10/31/2004 12:00:00AM
	2,337	$68.00	11/7/2004 12:00:00AM	11/13/2004 12:00:00AM
	2,402	$185.20	11/22/2004 12:00:00AM	11/23/2004 12:00:00AM
	2,528	$136.47	12/24/2004 12:00:00AM	12/24/2004 12:00:00AM
	2,640	$2,939.85	1/26/2005 12:00:00AM	1/26/2005 12:00:00AM
	2,659	$659.70	1/30/2005 12:00:00AM	2/1/2005 12:00:00AM
	2,682	$931.05	2/2/2005 12:00:00AM	2/4/2005 12:00:00AM
	2,687	$27.00	2/4/2005 12:00:00AM	2/10/2005 12:00:00AM
	2,772	$2,294.55	2/28/2005 12:00:00AM	3/5/2005 12:00:00AM
	2,900	$5,549.40	4/9/2005 12:00:00AM	4/16/2005 12:00:00AM
	2,982	$63.90	4/29/2005 12:00:00AM	5/2/2005 12:00:00AM
2				
	1,303	$1,505.10	2/18/2003 12:00:00AM	3/2/2003 12:00:00AM
	1,145	$27.00	1/6/2004 12:00:00AM	1/17/2004 6:33:11PM
	1,171	$479.85	1/14/2004 12:00:00AM	1/14/2004 2:39:50AM
	1,233	$139.48	1/27/2004 12:00:00AM	1/29/2004 1:12:05PM
	1,254	$2,497.05	2/3/2004 12:00:00AM	2/4/2004 3:51:39PM
	1,256	$70.50	2/4/2004 12:00:00AM	2/4/2004 9:27:33AM

Adding a Text Object to a Report

1. Select **Insert.**

2. Select **Text Object.**

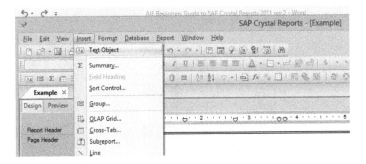

3. Draw the Text Object box on any section.

4. Type the text.

5. Resize the Text Object box if necessary.

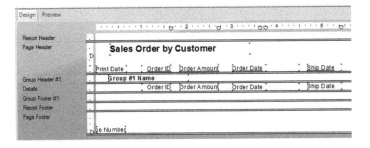

6. Select **Preview** to view the report.

7. Reposition or change the text, font, size or color if needed.

Sales Order by Customer

5/3/2013	Order ID	Order Amount	Order Date	Ship Date
1				
	1,366	$764.85	2/27/2003 12:00:00AM	2/28/2003 12:00:00AM
	1	$41.90	12/2/2003 12:00:00AM	12/10/2003 5:32:23PM
	1,033	$3,520.30	12/8/2003 12:00:00AM	12/20/2003 5:23:15PM
	1,041	$764.85	12/11/2003 12:00:00AM	12/13/2003 11:29:38AM
	1,092	$42.00	12/24/2003 12:00:00AM	12/26/2003 6:43:59AM
	1,143	$62.33	1/6/2004 12:00:00AM	1/8/2004 4:29:38AM
	1,246	$3,884.25	1/30/2004 12:00:00AM	1/30/2004 5:31:27PM
	1,296	$6,682.98	2/16/2004 12:00:00AM	2/16/2004 12:00:00AM
	1,387	$1,515.35	3/1/2004 12:00:00AM	3/1/2004 12:00:00AM
	1,717	$70.50	6/14/2004 12:00:00AM	6/15/2004 12:00:00AM

Adding a Picture or Graphic Image

1. Go to the **Design** tab.

2. Resize the target area to insert the graphic file.

    a. Move the cursor to the bottom line of the section to insert the graphic file.

    b. Hold down the left-mouse click when the cursor changes.

    c. Expand the area by moving the mouse down.

3. Select **Insert.**

4. Select **Picture.**

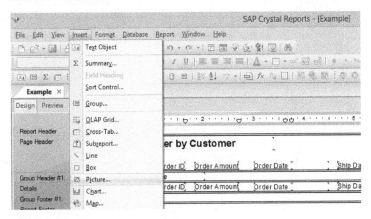

5. Select the graphic filename.

6. Select **Open.**

7. Position the graphic image by moving the square guide to the desired location.

8. Click to place the graphic image.

9. Resize the graphic image.

10. Resize the section, if necessary.

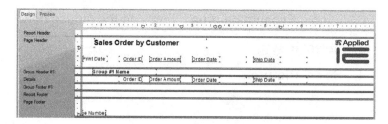

11. Select **Preview** tab to view the report.

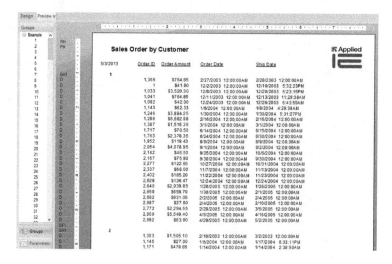

Chapter 5: Report Filters and Parameters

Data selection to show on reports can be controlled by using report filters and/or report parameters. Report developers will initially create a general report using report filters and include a report option for users to enter report parameters such as date range or customer name.

Filters vs. Parameters

Report Filter via Select Expert

Filters select records based on a set of rules established by a report developer. The set of rules identify data fields that meet certain criteria or condition such as <Fieldname> = "Yes". Filter conditions are "fixed" or embedded as part of the report and cannot be changed by report users.

Report Parameter

Parameters are "user-defined" conditions that can change each time a report is executed. The report developer creates "parameter fields" to enable users to control the type of data to show on the report. A report date range prompting a user each time a report is executed is an example of a report parameter.

Filtering Records to Display

1. Select **Report.**

2. Click on **Select Expert.**

3. Select **Record.**

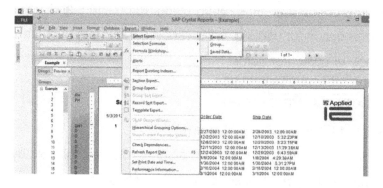

... Another approach is ...

1. Click on **Select Expert icon** pull down menu.

2. Select **Record.**

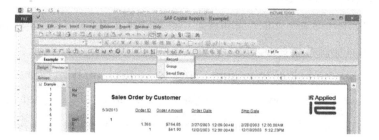

3. Select field *Orders.Order Amount* to filter.

4. Select **OK.**

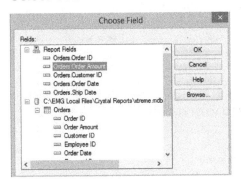

5. Select the filter command such as *is greater than.*

6. Enter the value such as **1000.**

7. Select **OK.**

8. Select **Use Saved Data** to view previously downloaded data or **Refresh Data** to download new set of data.

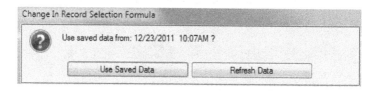

9. Select **Preview** to view report.

Sales Order by Customer

5/3/2013	Order ID	Order Amount	Order Date	Ship Date
1				
	1,033	$3,520.30	12/8/2003 12:00:00AM	12/20/2003 5:23:15PM
	1,246	$3,884.25	1/30/2004 12:00:00AM	1/30/2004 5:31:27PM
	1,296	$6,682.98	2/16/2004 12:00:00AM	2/16/2004 12:00:00AM
	1,387	$1,515.35	3/1/2004 12:00:00AM	3/1/2004 12:00:00AM
	1,763	$2,378.35	6/24/2004 12:00:00AM	6/30/2004 12:00:00AM
	2,054	$4,078.95	9/1/2004 12:00:00AM	9/2/2004 12:00:00AM
	2,640	$2,939.85	1/26/2005 12:00:00AM	1/26/2005 12:00:00AM
	2,772	$2,294.55	2/28/2005 12:00:00AM	3/5/2005 12:00:00AM
	2,900	$5,549.40	4/9/2005 12:00:00AM	4/16/2005 12:00:00AM
2				
	1,303	$1,505.10	2/18/2003 12:00:00AM	3/2/2003 12:00:00AM
	1,254	$2,497.05	2/3/2004 12:00:00AM	2/4/2004 3:51:39PM
	1,288	$8,819.55	2/12/2004 12:00:00AM	2/12/2004 12:00:00AM
	1,633	$5,879.70	5/21/2004 12:00:00AM	5/23/2004 12:00:00AM
	1,743	$1,489.05	6/20/2004 12:00:00AM	6/23/2004 12:00:00AM
	1,883	$3,526.70	7/21/2004 12:00:00AM	7/27/2004 12:00:00AM
	1,916	$1,131.25	7/29/2004 12:00:00AM	7/30/2004 12:00:00AM
	1,915	$1,086.05	7/29/2004 12:00:00AM	8/3/2004 12:00:00AM
	1,941	$5,879.70	8/6/2004 12:00:00AM	8/14/2004 12:00:00AM
	2,243	$1,523.35	10/19/2004 12:00:00AM	10/19/2004 12:00:00AM
	2,242	$8,819.55	10/19/2004 12:00:00AM	10/19/2004 12:00:00AM
	2,606	$1,083.04	1/15/2005 12:00:00AM	1/15/2005 12:00:00AM
	2,652	$2,429.10	1/29/2005 12:00:00AM	2/5/2005 12:00:00AM
	2,653	$2,451.85	1/29/2005 12:00:00AM	2/8/2005 12:00:00AM
	2,777	$1,529.70	3/1/2005 12:00:00AM	3/8/2005 12:00:00AM
	2,969	$3,185.42	4/26/2005 12:00:00AM	5/1/2005 12:00:00AM

Creating Parameter Fields

1. Open Field Explorer.

2. Right-Mouse click Parameter Fields.

3. Select **New.**

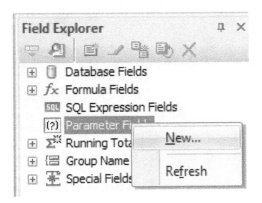

4. Enter Name of the Parameter field such as **Date Range.**

5. Select the parameter **Type** to match the data field type. See Tip: Browse Data.

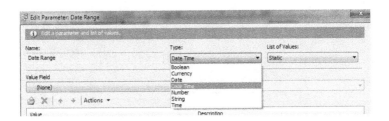

6. For a date range, select **Option: Allow Range Values** to **True.**

7. Select **OK.**

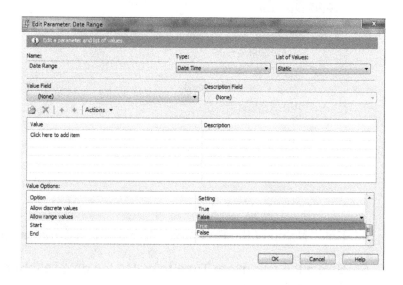

Setting Up a Report Parameter

1. Select **Report.**

2. Click on **Select Expert.**

3. Select **Record.**

4. Select **New** Tab.

5. Select field ***Orders.Order Date*** to set parameter.

6. Select **OK.**

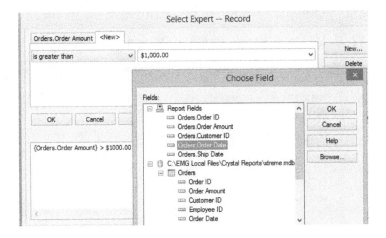

7. Set condition to "**is equal to**".

8. Go to pull-down menu to select user created parameter
    field that starts with a "**?**". If you do not find the parameter
    field, the parameter field does not have the same field type
    as the selected field. Go to the parameter field and
    change the field type.

9. Select **OK** to save.

10. Select **Preview** to view or run report.

11. Pop-up menu appears for the parameter range.

12. Enter Date Range **01/01/2004** to **12/30/2004.**

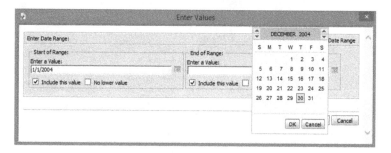

TIP: Browse Data

Examine the *Field Type* and *Browse Data* to learn more about the data set in a field.

1. Open **Field Explorer.**

2. Right-Mouse click on the field.

3. Select **Browse Data.**

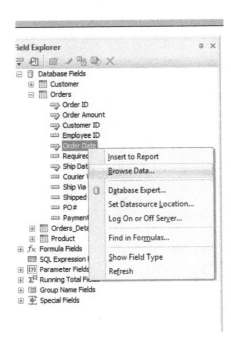

4. View sample data.

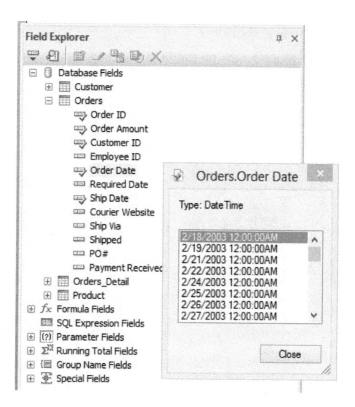

Chapter 6: Basic Math Functions

Adding Field Data with Running Totals Fields

Creating a Running Total Field

1. Open the **Field Explorer.**

2. Right-Mouse click Running Totals Fields.

3. Select **New.**

4. Type the **Running Total Name.**

5. Click on the field **Orders.Order Amount** .

6. Click the ">" icon to select the field name.

7. Select the "Type of Summary" such as **sum.**

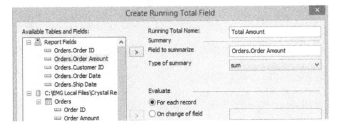

8. For the **Reset** option, select **On Change of Group.**

9. Select **OK** when done.

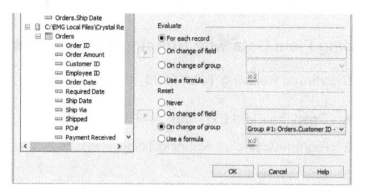

10. Notice the new field **Total Amount** under "Running Total Fields".

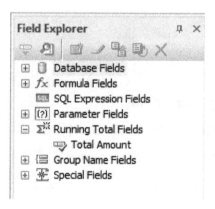

Inserting a Running Total Field

1. Drag the running total field in the Group Footer #1 section.

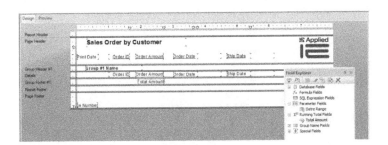

2. Select **Preview** to view report.

Sales Order by Customer

5/3/2013	Order ID	Order Amount	Order Date	Ship Date
1				
	1,246	$3,884.25	1/30/2004 12:00:00AM	1/30/2004 5:31:27PM
	1,296	$6,682.98	2/16/2004 12:00:00AM	2/16/2004 12:00:00AM
	1,387	$1,515.35	3/1/2004 12:00:00AM	3/1/2004 12:00:00AM
	1,763	$2,378.35	6/24/2004 12:00:00AM	6/30/2004 12:00:00AM
	2,054	$4,078.95	9/1/2004 12:00:00AM	9/2/2004 12:00:00AM
		$18,539.88		
2				
	1,254	$2,497.05	2/3/2004 12:00:00AM	2/4/2004 3:51:39PM
	1,288	$8,819.55	2/12/2004 12:00:00AM	2/12/2004 12:00:00AM
	1,633	$5,879.70	5/21/2004 12:00:00AM	5/23/2004 12:00:00AM
	1,743	$1,489.05	6/20/2004 12:00:00AM	6/23/2004 12:00:00AM
	1,883	$3,526.70	7/21/2004 12:00:00AM	7/27/2004 12:00:00AM
	1,916	$1,131.25	7/29/2004 12:00:00AM	7/30/2004 12:00:00AM
	1,915	$1,086.05	7/29/2004 12:00:00AM	8/3/2004 12:00:00AM
	1,941	$5,879.70	8/6/2004 12:00:00AM	8/14/2004 12:00:00AM
	2,243	$1,523.35	10/19/2004 12:00:00AM	10/19/2004 12:00:00AM
	2,242	$8,819.55	10/19/2004 12:00:00AM	10/19/2004 12:00:00AM
		$40,651.95		
3				

Adding Formula Fields

Creating a Simple Formula Filed

1. Open **Field Explorer.**

2. Right-Mouse click Formula Fields.

3. Select **New .**

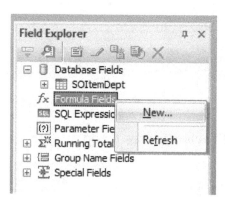

4. Enter Formula Name such as *Exchange $.*

5. Select **OK.**

6. Type the "**{**" to display the table options.

7. Select the table **Orders.**

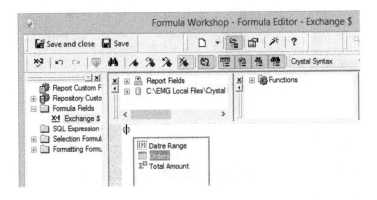

8. Select the field **Order Amount.**

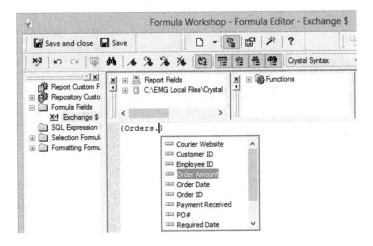

9. Type the math operation **{Orders.Order Amount} * 5**.

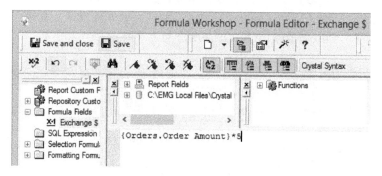

10. Select the [X-2] icon or **Alt-C** to verify formula.

11. Select **OK.**

12. Select **Save and Close.**

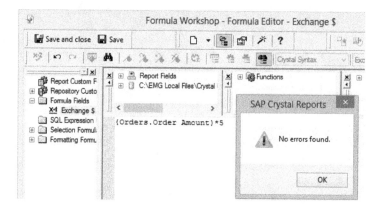

13. Notice the new field *Exchange $* under the Formula Fields.

Sales Order by Customer

Order ID	Order Amount	Order Date	Ship Date
1,246	$3,884.25	01/30/2004	01/30/2004
1,296	$6,682.98	02/16/2004	02/16/2004
1,387	$1,515.35	03/01/2004	03/01/2004
1,763	$2,378.35	06/24/2004	06/30/2004
2,054	$4,078.95	09/01/2004	09/02/2004
	$18,539.88		
1,254	$2,497.05	02/03/2004	02/04/2004
1,288	$8,819.55	02/12/2004	02/12/2004
1,633	$5,879.70	05/21/2004	05/23/2004
1,743	$1,489.05	06/20/2004	06/23/2004
1,883	$3,526.70	07/21/2004	07/27/2004
1,916	$1,131.25	07/29/2004	07/30/2004
1,915	$1,086.05	07/29/2004	08/03/2004

Field Explorer

- Database Fields
  - Orders
- Formula Fields
  - Exchange $
  - SQL Expression Fields
- Parameter Fields
  - Datre Range
- Running Total Fields
  - Total Amount
- Group Name Fields
- Special Fields

Creating an If-Then-Else Formula Filed

1. Open **Field Explorer.**

2. Right-Mouse click **Formula Fields**.

3. Select **New.**

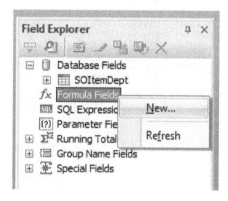

4. Enter Formula Name such as *Sale Type.*

5. Select **OK.**

6. Enter the Formula .

If {@Exchange $} > 10000 Then "A" Else "B"

7. Select [X-2] check icon to confirm formula is correct.

8. Select **Save and Close** to save formula.

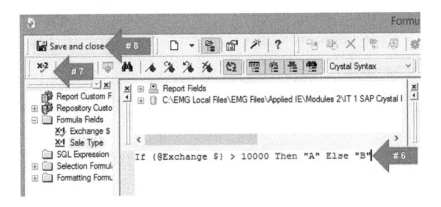

Inserting Formula Fields

1. Select and drag the formula fields in the Details section.
   - Select fields *Exchange $* and *Sale Type.*

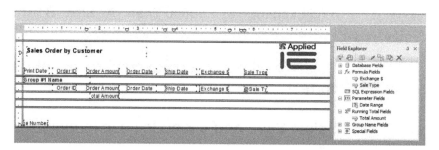

2. Select **Preview** tab to view report.

Sales Order by Customer

10/31/2013	Order ID	Order Amount	Order Date	Ship Date	Exchange $	Sale Type
1						
	1,246	$3,884.25	01/30/2004	01/30/2004	$19,421.25	A
	1,296	$6,682.98	02/16/2004	02/16/2004	$33,414.90	A
	1,387	$1,515.35	03/01/2004	03/01/2004	$7,576.75	B
	1,763	$2,378.35	06/24/2004	06/30/2004	$11,891.75	A
	2,054	$4,078.95	09/01/2004	09/02/2004	$20,394.75	A
		$18,539.88				
2						
	1,254	$2,497.05	02/03/2004	02/04/2004	$12,485.25	A
	1,288	$8,819.55	02/12/2004	02/12/2004	$44,097.75	A
	1,633	$5,879.70	05/21/2004	05/23/2004	$29,398.50	A
	1,743	$1,489.05	06/20/2004	06/23/2004	$7,445.25	B
	1,883	$3,526.70	07/21/2004	07/27/2004	$17,633.50	A
	1,915	$1,086.05	07/29/2004	08/03/2004	$5,430.25	B
	1,916	$1,131.25	07/29/2004	07/30/2004	$5,656.25	B
	1,941	$5,879.70	08/06/2004	08/14/2004	$29,398.50	A
	2,243	$1,523.35	10/19/2004	10/19/2004	$7,616.75	B
	2,242	$8,819.55	10/19/2004	10/19/2004	$44,097.75	A
		$40,651.95				
3						
	1,294	$5,879.70	02/15/2004	02/15/2004	$29,398.50	A
	1,357	$1,664.70	02/26/2004	02/26/2004	$8,323.50	B
	1,964	$1,721.25	08/12/2004	08/13/2004	$8,606.25	B
	2,112	$5,545.42	09/16/2004	09/24/2004	$27,727.10	A
	2,162	$1,019.70	09/28/2004	09/30/2004	$5,098.50	B
		$15,830.77				

Chapter 7: Summary Reports

Creating a Summary Report

Develop reports to show summaries, such as the totals and averages, for a certain time period or grouping of data. Report developers can provide access to users to "drill-down" to show the details of each summary.

Hiding Report Details with Drill Down

1. Right-Mouse click the Details section.

2. Select **Hide (Drill-Down OK)** or select **Suppress (No Drill Down)** to disable drill-down option.

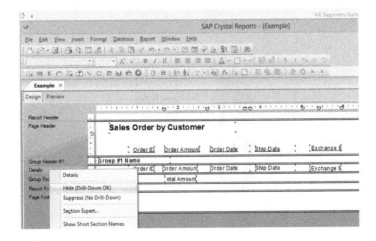

3. Select **Preview** tab to view report.

Sales Order by Customer

	Order ID	Order Amount	Order Date	Ship Date	Exchange $
1					
		$18,539.88			
2					
		$40,651.95			
3					
		$15,830.77			
4					
		$62,905.99			
5					

4. Double-click the Department name to drill-down or view details of summary.

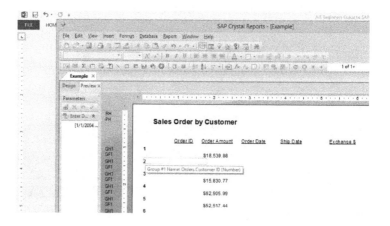

5. Notice a new tab with the drill-down results.

6. Select "**x**" on the details tab to close the view.

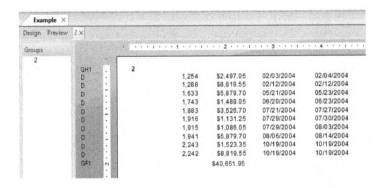

Refining the Summary Report

1. Click on Design tab.

2. Move the *Group# 1 Name* from the Group Header section to the Group Footer section.

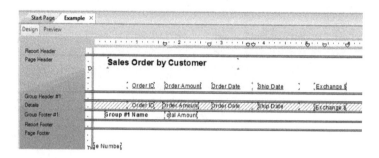

3. Move the field titles or column header from the Page Header section to the Group Header section.

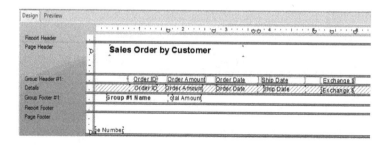

4. Copy the "Order Amount" text.

    a. Right-click on the text.

    b. Select Copy.

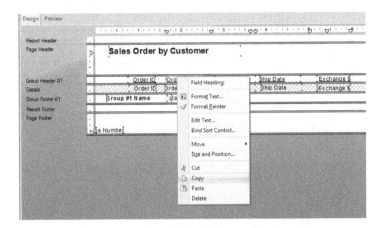

5. Paste "Order Amount" text to the Page Header section.

    a. Right-mouse click on the Page Header section.

    b. Select Paste.

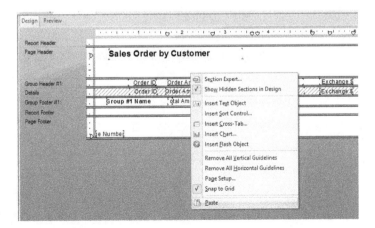

6. Position "Order Amount" text.

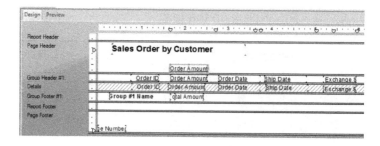

7. Add "Customer ID" text to label column header.

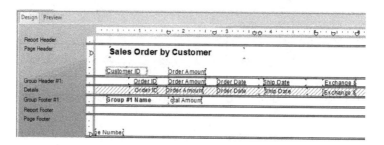

8. Set Group Header to Hide (Drill-Down OK).

   a. Right-mouse click on Group Header section.

   b. Select Hide (Drill-Down OK).

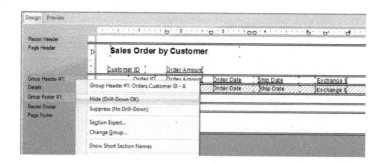

9. Select Preview tab.

Sales Order by Customer

Customer ID	Order Amount
1	$18,539.88
2	$40,651.95
3	$15,830.77
4	$62,905.99
5	$52,517.44
6	$36,343.95
7	$15,777.99
8	$14,666.16
9	$21,888.09
10	$26,569.08
11	$32,857.62
12	$45,771.49
13	$27,542.57
14	$23,014.10
15	$27,434.90

10. Double-click on Customer ID record to view details.

Order ID	Order Amount	Order Date	Ship Date	Exchange $
1,254	$2,497.05	02/03/2004	02/04/2004	$12,485.25
1,288	$8,819.55	02/12/2004	02/12/2004	$44,097.75
1,633	$5,879.70	05/21/2004	05/23/2004	$29,398.50
1,743	$1,489.05	06/20/2004	06/23/2004	$7,445.25
1,883	$3,526.70	07/21/2004	07/27/2004	$17,633.50
1,916	$1,131.25	07/29/2004	07/30/2004	$5,656.25
1,915	$1,086.05	07/29/2004	08/03/2004	$5,430.25
1,941	$5,879.70	08/06/2004	08/14/2004	$29,398.50
2,243	$1,523.35	10/19/2004	10/19/2004	$7,616.75
2,242	$8,819.55	10/19/2004	10/19/2004	$44,097.75
2	$40,651.95			

Chapter 8: Using Multiple Data Tables

Identifying Data Tables Required for a Report

1. Create a pencil draft of the proposed report to create.

2. Identify the data fields required for the report.

3. Determine if the fields can be found in a single data table in the Tables or Views.

4. Identify the tables containing the required data fields.

5. Identify common data fields to link or connect multiple data fields. These common fields are also known as key fields.

Selecting Data Tables

1. Select **File.**

2. Select **New.**

3. Select **Standard Report.**

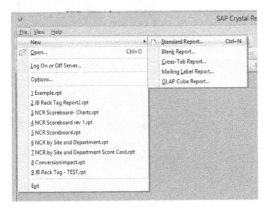

4. Select **Data Source.**

5. Expand to the table location.

6. Expand to view tables.

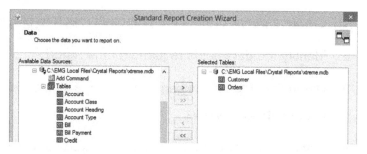

7. Select **Tables.**

8. Click on **Next.**

9. Verify the field links of the tables. The automatic detection of linking fields require user review.

10. Select **Finish.**

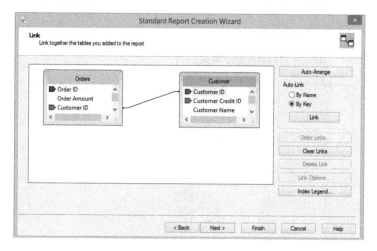

Linking Fields

Common key fields are required to link tables as shown below. In some cases, there may be multiple key fields that are required to logically connect tables.

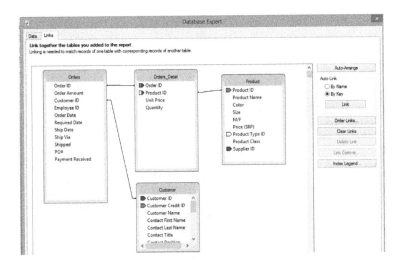

Color-coded markings next to key fields indicate the indexing priority of the table. As much as possible, select indexed fields for quicker data access.

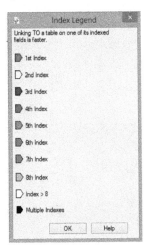

Chapter 9: Adding a Chart

Creating a Basic Chart

1. Click on the **Design** tab.

2. Expand the **Report Footer** to allocate space for a chart.

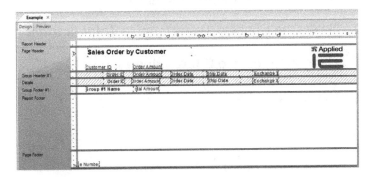

3. Select **Insert.**

4. Select **Chart.**

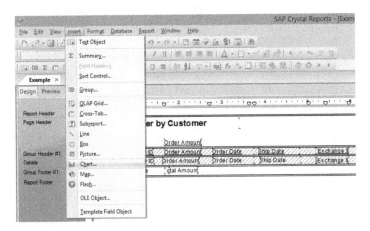

5. Position the guide box at the Page Footer even if the box is larger than the allocated space.

6. The Chart Expert menu is displayed.

7. Select *Orders.Ship_Date.*

8. Click on ">" next to **On change of**.

9. Select the Running Totals formula *Total Amount.*

10. Click on ">" next to **Show value(s).**

11. Select **OK.**

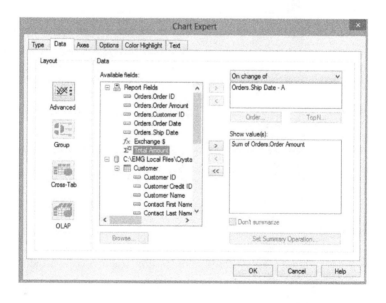

12. Select **Preview.**

13. Go to last page Report Footer to view chart.

    Notice the chart displaying the total Order Amount per ship date with a Legend Box on the right.

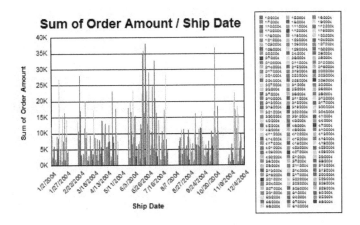

Changing Daily Amount to a Monthly Amount

1. Right-mouse click on chart to display menu.

2. Select **Chart Expert.**

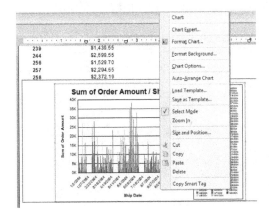

3. Select **Data** tab.

4. Select On change of field *Orders.Ship_Date.*

5. Change **The section will be printed:** option from **for each day** to **for each month.**

6. Select **OK.**

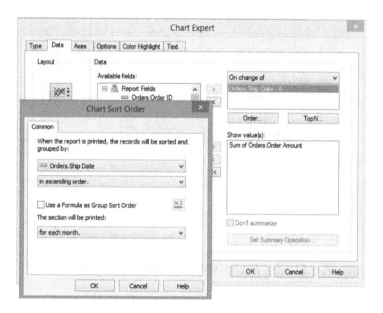

7. Chart displays Total Order Amount per Month.

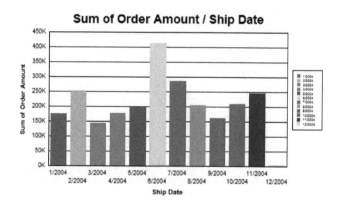

Removing the Legend Box

1. Right-mouse click on the chart area to display the menu.

2. Select Chart Expert.

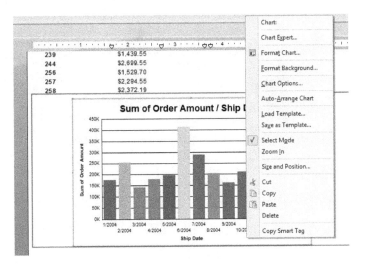

3. Select **Options** tab.

4. Unselect or uncheck the **Show Legend** box.

5. Select **OK.**

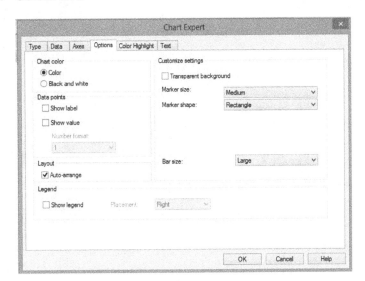

6. View the chart without the Legend Box.

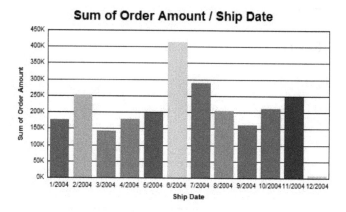

Changing Titles and Labels

1. Right-mouse click on the chart area to display the menu.
2. Select **Chart Expert.**

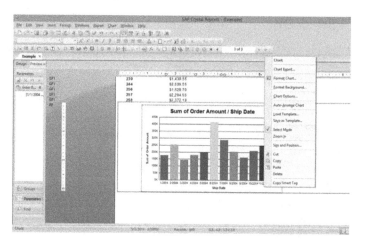

3. Select the **Text** tab.

4. Uncheck the applicable **Auto-Text** check box.

5. Enter the titles and labels as shown below.

6. Select OK.

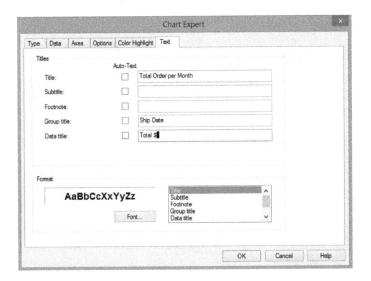

7. View the updated chart.

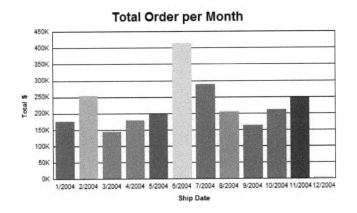

Changing the Chart Type

1. Right-mouse click on the chart area to display the menu.

2. Select **Chart Expert.**

3. At the Type tab, select **Line** and the appropriate Line Chart type.

4. Select **OK.**

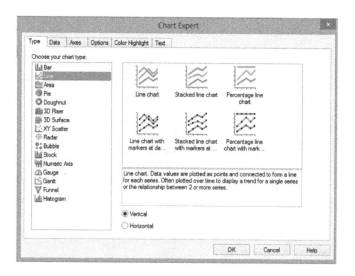

5. View the updated chart .

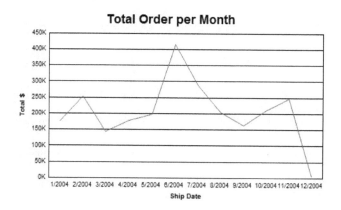

Chapter 10: Cross-Tabs

Cross Tab is an easy-to-use utility to create a detailed data grid or a summary data grid.

Creating a Cross-Tab

1. Select **Insert** menu.
2. Select **Cross-Tab.**

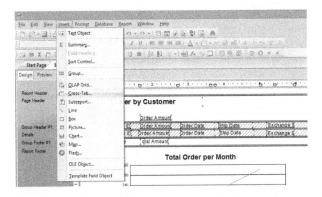

3. Position and click guide box to position Cross-Tab.
4. Right-mouse click on Cross-Tab to open menu.
5. Select **Cross-Tab Expert.**

6. Select *Orders.Order_Date.*

7. Select "**>**" on Rows.

8. Select formula *Total Amount.*

9. Select "**>**" on Summary Fields.

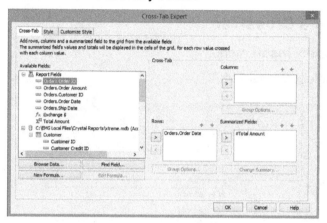

10. Select **Preview.**

Notice that the Total Amount listed by day.

	Total
Total	$4,317,395.77
1/2/2004	$3,842.55
1/5/2004	$2,654.56
1/6/2004	$1,830.35
1/8/2004	$5,879.70

Summarizing Data

1. Right-mouse click on Cross-Tab to open menu.

2. Select **Cross-Tab Expert.**

3. Click on *Orders.Order_Date.*

4. Select **Group Option.**

5. Click on **Row will be printed** pull down menu.

6. Select summary period such as **for each month.**

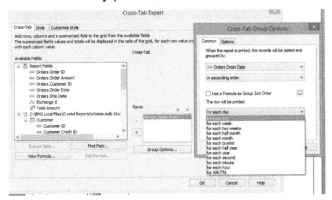

7. Select **OK** on Cross-Tab Group Options.

8. Select **OK** on Cross-Tab Expert to view result.

	Total
Total	$159,569.76
1/2004	$1,409.55
2/2004	$2,416.80
3/2004	$5,952.85
4/2004	$4,288.90

Adding Data Columns

1. Right-mouse click on Cross-Tab to open menu.

2. Select **Cross-Tab Expert.**

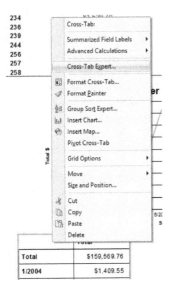

3. Select *Orders.Customer_ID.*

4. Select "**>**" on Columns.

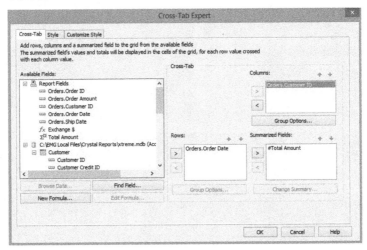

5. Select **OK** to view result. The cross-tab shows total monthly amount per customer ID.

	Total	1	2	3	4	5
Total	$8,051,160.91	$18,539.88	$40,651.95	$15,830.77	$62,905.99	$52,517.44
1/2004	$195,117.54	$3,884.25	$0.00	$0.00	$0.00	$11,792.66
2/2004	$309,780.53	$10,567.23	$11,316.60	$7,544.40	$0.00	$28,675.52
3/2004	$331,301.39	$12,082.58	$0.00	$0.00	$3,147.21	$34,439.44
4/2004	$387,327.71	$0.00	$0.00	$0.00	$18,716.16	$0.00

Chapter 11: Intermediate Skills and Tips

This chapter is a collection of commonly used features for intermediate users of Crystal Reports. It is recommended that readers be proficient on the fundamental skills described in Chapters 1 to 9 prior to reading this chapter.

Parameter Field Options

Value Field

Introduction Use this option to create a Pick List of items for a report user.

Options
1. Select Value Field.
2. Select Actions.
3. Select Append all database values.

Value Options

Prompt Text Option to change the default message .

Default Value Option to set a default value for the user.

Allow Multiple Values Option for the user to select multiple values from a pick list or enter the values manually.

Set Allow Multiple Values = True.

Value Options:	
Option	Setting
Allow multiple values	False

Allow Range Values Option for the user to enter a minimum and maximum value. Set Allow range values = True.

Value Options:	
Option	Setting
Allow discrete values	False
Allow range values	True

Change Date-Time parameter to Date Only

Introduction   Setting up a parameter requires the field type to be the same as the field used in Select Expert. With a Time parameter included, there is risk of excluding data in a specified date range. Changing the parameter from Date-Time to Date assures complete data extraction and simplifies the Date Range prompt.

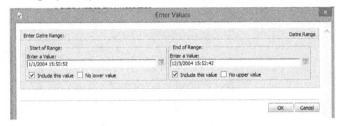

Procedure

1. Set up the parameter field to match the Date-Time field type.

2. Add the data field and parameter field in **Select Expert.**

3. Edit the Parameter field Type from Date-Time to **Date.**

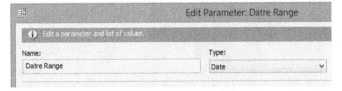

4. Change the **Allow Range Values** = True.

5. Select **OK.**

Result

Field Format

Change Font Color Based on a Formula Condition

Introduction   The font color can be changed when a certain condition in a formula is satisfied.

Procedure
1. Right-mouse click on field to show menu.
2. Select Format Field.
3. Select Font tab.
4. Click on [X-2] icon to the right of Color:
5. Enter the formula such as

   If {#Total Amount}<20000 then crRed else crBlack

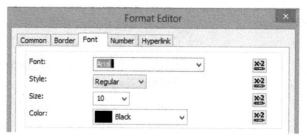

6. Select Save and Close
7. Select OK

Result

Sales Order by Customer

Customer ID	Order Amount
1	$18,539.88
2	$40,651.95
3	$15,830.77
4	$62,905.99
5	$52,517.44
6	$36,343.95
7	$15,777.99
8	$14,666.16
9	$21,888.09

Suppressing a Field Value

Introduction   A formula or a data field can be suppressed, or not be displayed, based on a set parameter.

Procedure
1. Right-mouse click on field to show menu.
2. Select Format Field.
3. Select Common tab
4. Click on [X-2] icon to the right of the Suppress checkbox.
5. Enter the formula such as

   {#Total Amount}<20000

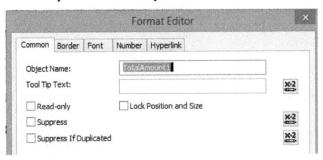

6. Select Save and Close.
7. Select OK.

Result   **Sales Order by Customer**

Customer ID	Order Amount
1	
2	$40,651.95
3	
4	$62,905.99
5	$52,517.44
6	$36,343.95
7	
8	
9	$21,888.09
10	$26,569.08
11	$32,857.62
12	$45,771.49

Formulas

Adding Text Fields

Syntax   {TableName.Fieldname1} + {TableName.FieldName2}

Example   If   {TableName.Fieldname1} = "John"
                      {TableName.FieldName2} = "Smith"

Result   JohnSmith

Adding Text Fields and Fixed Characters

Syntax   {TableName.Fieldname1} + "-" +{TableName.FieldName2}

Example   If   {TableName.Fieldname1} = "John"
                      {TableName.FieldName2} = "Smith"

Result   John-Smith

Converting a Number Field to Text / String

Syntax   ToText (x, y, z)

x = {TableName.Fieldname}
y = Decimal Positions such as 0, 1, 2,…
z = Thousands separator such as a ","

Example   If   {TableName.Fieldname} = 1234.56

(1) ToText ({TableName.Fieldname},1,",")
(2) ToText ({TableName.Fieldname},0,"")

Result   (1) 1,234.5
(2) 1234

Selecting the First or Last Characters of a Field

Syntax   LEFT (x,y)

RIGHT (x,y)

x = String or a TableName.Fieldname

y = Number of characters to extracted

Example   (1) LEFT ("AAA-BB-CCC",5)

(2) RIGHT ("AAA-BB-CCC",5)

Result   (1) AAA-B
(2) B-CCC

Extracting a Numerical Value from a Date Field

Syntax   DatePart (w, x)

w = Interval Type

x = {TableName.Fieldname}

Interval type value	Description
yyyy	Year value
q	Quarter value 1, 2, 3 or 4
m	Month value 1 to 12
y	Day of year 1 to 365 or 366 in a leap year
d	Day of the month 1 to 31
w	Day of week value 1 to 7 with Sunday as Day 1 as the default
ww	Week value of year 1 to 53
h	Hour value 0 to 23
n	Minute value 0 to 59
s	Seconds value 0 to 59

Example   If   {TableName.Fieldname} = 10/02/2013 5:31:27PM

(1) DatePart("yyyy", {TableName.Fieldname})

(2) DatePart("q", {TableName.Fieldname})

(3) DatePart("m", {TableName.Fieldname})

Result   (1) 2013

(2) 4

(3) 10

Splitting or Selecting a Segment of a Delimited Field

Introduction   A Delimited field is a single data field containing multiple data components separated by a character (delimiter) such as a "-" or "|".

Syntax   Split (x,y) [n]

x = {TableName.Fieldname}

y = Delimiter or separator character such as "-"

n = The data component starting from the left

Example   If   {TableName.Fieldname} = "AAA-BB-CCC"

(1) Split ({TableName.Fieldname},"-")[2]
(2) Split ({TableName.Fieldname},"-")[1]

Result   (1) BB
(2) AAA

Data in Field Is One Of

Introduction Condition is True if the fieldname is an item in the data set.

Syntax {TableName.Fieldname} in ["a", "b", "c",...]

a = Text value 1

b = Text value 2

c = Text value 3

Example If {TableName.Fieldname} in ["A5","Z6"]

Then 25

Else 40

(1) {TableName.Fieldname} = "TX"
(2) {TableName.Fieldname} = "Z6"
(3) {TableName.Fieldname} = "A4"
(4) {TableName.Fieldname} = "A5"

Result (1) 40
(2) 25
(3) 40
(4) 25

Data in Field Is Not One Of

Introduction   Condition is True if the fieldname is NOT an item in the data set.

Syntax   Not {TableName.Fieldname} in ["a", "b", "c",...]

a = Text value 1

b = Text value 2

c = Text value 3

Example   If   Not {TableName.Fieldname} in ["A5","Z6"]

Then 25

Else 40

(1) {TableName.Fieldname} = "TX"
(2) {TableName.Fieldname} = "Z6"
(3) {TableName.Fieldname} = "A4"
(4) {TableName.Fieldname} = "A5"

Result   (1) 25
(2) 40
(3) 25
(4) 40

Evaluating a Null Field

Introduction   A Null field is a condition where no data is assigned to the field of a record. A zero value is not the same as a Null value.

Syntax   IsNull {TableName.Fieldname}

Example   If   IsNull {TableName.Fieldname}

      Then "True"

      Else "False"

      (1) {TableName.Fieldname} = 0
      (2) {TableName.Fieldname} = ""
      (3) {TableName.Fieldname} = 5

Result   (1) False
      (2) True
      (3) False

Evaluating Field that is NOT a Null Value

Syntax   Not IsNull {TableName.Fieldname}

Example   If   Not IsNull {TableName.Fieldname}

      Then "True"

      Else "False"

      (4) {TableName.Fieldname} = 0
      (5) {TableName.Fieldname} = ""
      (6) {TableName.Fieldname} = 5

Result   (4) True
      (5) False
      (6) True

Running Total Field

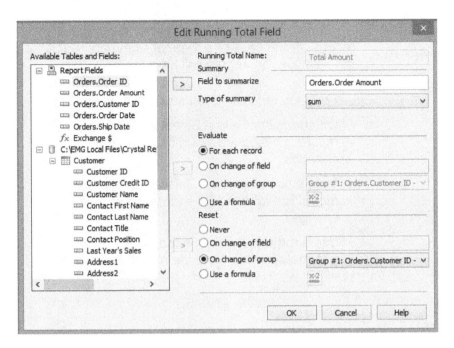

Type of Summary

Introduction   Use the pull-down menu to display the Type of Summary for the Running Total field.

Options

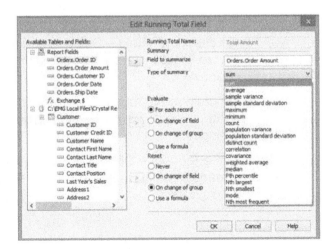

Evaluate Parameter

Introduction   A Running Total field defaults at evaluating every record. In the case of a Type of Summary = SUM, the field of every record will be added.

Options   o For each record – Evaluates every record.

o On change of Field – Select a sorted field. The record is evaluated when the sorted record value changes.

o On change of group – Select a Group. The record is evaluated when the Group value changes.

o Use a formula – Click on the [X-2] icon and enter a formula to determine the record to evaluate.

Reset Parameter

Introduction   Reset parameter determines when the Running Total value is reset to zero. The default value is Never.

Options   o Never – Does not reset to zero.

o On change of Field – Select a sorted field. The record is set to zero when the sorted record value changes.

o On change of group – Select a Group. The record is set to zero when the Group value changes.

o Use a formula – Click on the [X-2] icon and enter a formula to determine when to reset the value to zero.

Tips

Field Explorer Doesn't Launch

Issue   Field Explorer does not launch or display after selecting the Field Explorer icon or selecting View \ Field Explorer.

Corrective Action

1. Go to **View.**

2. Select **Toolbars.**

3. Check the box next to "Reset all toolbars and explorers on the next restart.".

4. Select **OK.**

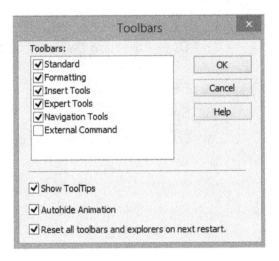

5. **Exit** Crystal Reports.

6. Launch Crystal Reports.

7. Open a report.

8. Launch Field Explorer.

Crystal Reports Crashes when Opening a Report File

Issue   An error message appears as soon as you open a
report file.

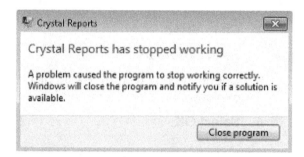

*Corrective
Action*

1. Open the report file on an older version as
    Crystal Reports XI.

2. Refresh the data.

3. Save the file.

4. Open the report file using current version.

Crystal Viewers

Developers use Crystal Reports to create report files that can be executed routinely using a crystal viewer. Executed reports pull updated data based on programmed data filters and user-defined parameters.

Software utilities, known as Crystal viewers, are available to enable Crystal Reports to run on a scheduled time, and deliver the reports via email, or direct to a printer. The reports can be delivered in various file formats such as PDF or MS Excel on a scheduled routine. I have used Logicity Pro by SaberLogic as a Crystal Reports viewer and robot utility to auto refresh performance scoreboards, send reports to a printer, generate PDF reports and store in a specific folder, run reports to print barcode labels, and encrypt Crystal Reports files.

SaberLogic offers a free version of Logicity to run Crystal Reports with full report functionality. It enables users to enter report parameters, and save the report as a PDF or MS Excel file. The reasonably priced Logicity Pro, provides the robot functionality to schedule tasks such as (1) auto refresh on a display, (2) send a report to a printer, (3) email reports, and (4) create PDF or MS Excel file reports and save to a designated folder. For more information, go to https://www.logicitysuite.com/.

Installing and Using Logicity

1. Download and install Logicity by SaberLogic.

    Note: Once installed, all Crystal Reports files (*.RPT) will
    execute using Logicity crystal viewer.

2. Double-click on the report file to launch the report using
    Logicity crystal viewer.

3. Enter User Parameters, if required.

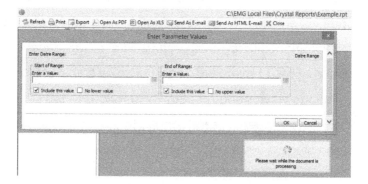

4. Use the report as designed.

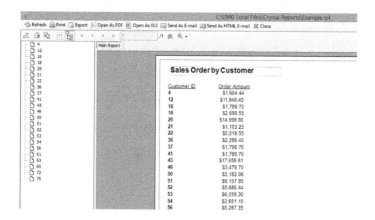

Logicity Crystal Viewer Screen Functions

C:\EMG Local Files\Crysta

Refresh | Print | Export | Open As PDF | Open As XLS | Send As E-mail | Send As HTML E-mail | Close

Refresh	Refresh the report data and if available, prompt for user parameters
Print	Send the report to a printer
Export	Save the report in a user-defined file type such as Excel, PDF, HTML or a Word file
Open to PDF	Display the report as a PDF file
Open as XLS	Display the report as a Microsoft© Excel file
Send as E-mail	Save the report in a user-defined file type such as Excel, PDF, HTML or a Word file, launch the default email utility, and attach the file to a new email.
Send As HTML E-mail	Save the report as an HTML file, launch the default email utility, and attach the file to a new email.
Close	Close the report file and Logicity crystal viewer

Automatically Refreshing a Report

1. Locate and launch **Logicity Solution Builder**.

2. Select **New** to build a scheduling application.

3. Select **Add Action.** Each scheduling application can contain multiple actions, such as refresh a report, print the report, and save report to a PDF file.

4. Enter the **Display Name** – name of the action or automation.

5. Select **Next**.

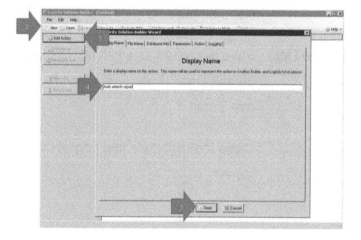

6. Select **Crystal Reports**.

7. Select **Browse** to locate the Crystal Reports file.

8. Select **Action** tab.

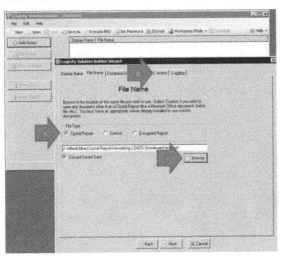

9. Select Action = **View**.

10. Select **Timed Interval** and enter a value.

11. Select **Next**.

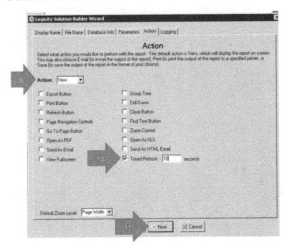

12. Select **Finish**.

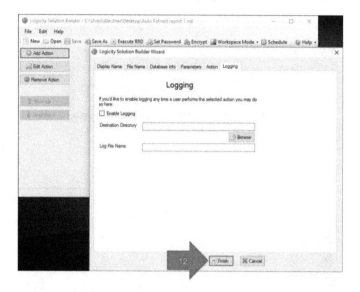

13. Select **Save As**.

14. Enter **filename**.

15. Select **Save**.

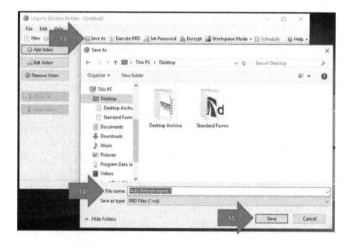

Launching a Scheduling Application

1. Locate RRD file.

2. Double-click to launch Crystal Reports with automated functions.

Learning Resources

There are numerous learning resources available for Crystal
Reports. Additional step-by-step learning tools in an interactive
session or a video presentation are available at the SAP
Community Network. Go to **http://scn.sap.com/docs/DOC-8514**
to access the step-by-step learning resource by SAP.

With the basic skills, the reader can progress at using the free user manual available from SAP, use the Help utility within Crystal Reports or search for Help topics available at the web.

SAP Crystal Reports User's Guide

1. Using a web browser, go to

   https://help.sap.com/viewer/p/SAP_CRYSTAL_REPORTS

2. Select **SAP Crystal Reports 2016 User Guide**

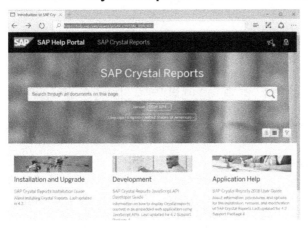

3. Browse the user manual.

Application Help Utility

1. Press F1 for Help utility

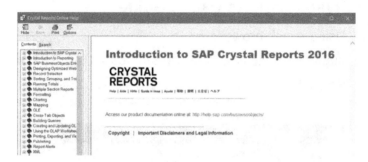

2. Select the Search tab to enter a specific topic

3. Select on the drop down menu or enter the topic to search

4. Press enter to list the topics

5. Double-click on the topic to display the Help details.

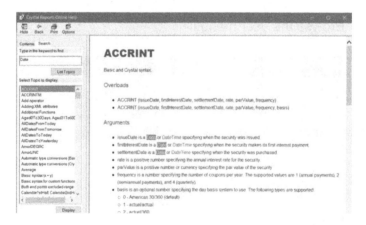

Web Community Help

1. Open a web browser

2. Type "Crystal Reports <help topic>" such as "Crystal Reports Running Totals"

3. Carefully select links and review Help notes

Index

CPSIA information can be obtained
at www.ICGtesting.com
Printed in the USA
FSHW020456060519
57876FS